Microsoft Office

Personal and Business

Table Of Contents

1. Introduction

1.1   Office 2013: What Have You Got?

1.2   Upgrading and Backward Compatibility

1.3   Microsoft Office 2013 on Windows RT Tablets

1.4   Different Flavors of Office 2013

1.5   Embracing the Cloud

2. Office 2013 and the Metro UI

2.1   Productivity for Fingers

2.2   What Is Metro?

2.3   Functional Changes Since Office 2010

3. What You Need to Know about Word 2013

3.1   Read Mode in Word 2013

3.5   Improvements to Collaboration

3.6   Define and Understand

4. Does Microsoft Excel Do Enough Already?

4.1   Recommended Charts

4.2   Quick Analysis

4.3   Suggested PivotTables

4.4   Power View for Power Users

5. PowerPoint 2013 – A New Dimension

5.4   Improvements to Slide Design

5.5   Collaboration Improvements in PowerPoint 2013

6. Microsoft Outlook - Redesigned

6.1   Inline Replies in Your Inbox

6.2   Calendar Improvements

6.3   People Are Contacts

6.4   Don't Touch It!

7. The Secret Weapon: OneNote

7.1   Making Notes the OneNote Way

7.2   Embedding Spreadsheets / One Note MX

8.   Office 2013 and Sky Drive

8.1   Integration with Sky Drive

9.   The Rest of Microsoft Office

9.1   Access

9.2   Publisher

9.3   Office 2013 Applications for Corporate Users

10.   Office 2013 – Should You Upgrade?

Appendix

1.   System Requirements

2.   Installing Office 2013

3.   Office Web Apps

1. Introduction

The world's most famous efficiency suite, Microsoft Office, is presently in its seventh variant with the arrival of Microsoft Office 2013, a cloud coordinated amendment of the product that comes finish with the new tile based UI earlier known as Metro (the look of which you will be acquainted with in the event that you have seen or utilized Windows 8).

Microsoft Office 2013 accompanies the greater part of the typical segment applications, the majority of which game luring new elements. Similarity with Windows is constrained contrasted and past Office adaptations, despite the fact that this new incarnation has touch screen bolster for tablet PCs and local Sky Drive cloud bolster for get to anyplace records.

Most strikingly, Microsoft is putting forth a few distinct kinds of Office 2013, most remarkably two membership based variants.

1.1 Office 2013: What Have You Got?

On the off chance that you need to compose reports and different archives, Microsoft Office 2013 is actually outfitted with the mother of all word processors, Word. Close by this, the spreadsheet application Exceed expectations, introduction programming PowerPoint and the prevalent note taking application OneNote are additionally included.

These four applications shape the center of every adaptation of Office 2013, while email and booking application Standpoint, desktop distributing instrument Distributer and database administration programming Access all stay accessible in Office 2013. InfoPath, Visio, Venture and Lync can likewise be added to the membership based Office 365 suites; you'll discover more about the diverse forms underneath.

1.2 Redesigning and In reverse Similarity

In the event that you wish to overhaul your present variant of Office to the new discharge, you should know that there is no "update way" – you essentially guarantee your records, word references and formats are spared, uninstall the old form and introduce Office 2013.

Distinctive variants are accessible, yet you can make a beeline for http://office.microsoft.com to download the trial adaptation of Office 365, which offers the best look at the refreshed applications.

Framework prerequisites for Microsoft Office 2013 can be found in Index 1.

Unfortunately, Office 2013 is not perfect with Windows XP or Windows Vista. At the season of composing, XP charges more than 40% of the piece of the pie of working frameworks more than 11 years after its dispatch; in the interim Vista holds an unassuming 6%, so 46% of the market can't redesign without first updating their working framework.

1.3 Microsoft Office 2013 on Windows RT Tablets

As you may have assembled, there are a few distinct variants of Microsoft Office 2013. The principle variant is for Windows PCs, despite the fact that there is an option form that comes included with Windows 8 RT gadgets.

On the off chance that you have acquired a Windows 8 tablet running this specific adaptation of the working framework (check the documentation to check whether your tablet has an ARM processor or the expression Windows RT is obvious) highlights Office 2013 Home and Understudy RT for no additional cost.

A few elements are cut back; to spare space, for example, layouts, cut craftsmanship and dialect packs must be downloaded while more seasoned document designs, outsider code for macros/VBA/ActiveX controls, PowerPoint portrayal, Exceed expectations information models and installed media record look in OneNote have all been barred.

By far most of things laid out in this manual apply to all renditions of Microsoft Office 2013.

1.4 Distinct Kinds of Office 2013

Notwithstanding the Windows 8 RT form of Office 2013, there are different bundles accessible, reasonable for various sorts of clients and prerequisites.

Office 2013 Home and Understudy incorporates the center quartet of utilizations, as recorded above, while Office 2013 Home and Business includes Viewpoint 2013. This guide will be most helpful to any individual who has obtained both of these two versions.

Moreover, a further bundle, Office 2013 Expert is accessible, which includes Distributer 2013 and Get to 2013. There are likewise four adaptations of Office

365, Microsoft's exceptional cloud-based office suite. Each of these has an alternate scope of utilizations and diverse permitting bundles.

Office 365 Home Premium offers bolster for five gadgets and incorporates Word, Exceed expectations, PowerPoint, OneNote, Viewpoint, Distributer and Access, with a discretionary Microsoft Extend 2013 part and a watcher for Visio documents. The other Office 365 suites include InfoPath and Lync 2013, and additionally the accompanying authorizing choices:

- *Office 365 Private venture Premium: 10 most extreme clients, 5 gadgets for each client.*
- *Office 365 ProPlus: 25 most extreme clients, 5 gadgets for every client.*
- *Office 365 Undertaking: Boundless number of greatest clients, 5 gadgets for every client.*

1.5   Embracing the Cloud

It isn't just Office 365 that makes utilization of the cloud, in any case. Regardless of whether you have acquired a solitary Office 2013 component or you're running the full suite, incorporation with Microsoft Sky Drive is incorporated.

Regardless of whether you're running Office 2013 on Windows 8 (where Sky Drive is completely incorporated with the OS), on Windows 7 (where Sky Drive has a downloadable segment that adds it to My

PC), the suite can be effortlessly associated with Sky Drive, empowering you to spare records to the cloud and open them later on in another area, or from another gadget.

You'll discover full points of interest on this in Area 8, Office 2013 and Sky Drive.

2.   Office 2013 and the Metro UI

Likewise with any reexamined arrival of programming, there are a few changes to the presence of Office 2013 that you may discover a need a bit of getting used to.

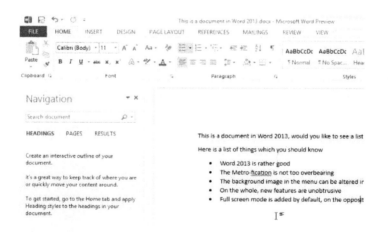

Composed with the new Metro UI (which has since been renamed to "Current" by Microsoft yet keeps on being alluded to as "Metro" by innovation writers), Office 2013 is like different applications and working frameworks utilizing Metro UI intended to be effortlessly utilized by fingertips.

Regardless of whether you're utilizing an on screen console on your Windows tablet gadget or indicating and clicking with a mouse in the conventional way, notwithstanding, you ought to experience little distinction in the client encounter.

2.1 Profitability for Fingers

After propelling Office 2013, you'll see that things are somewhat... square. This is because of the new UI, and can be best summed up by the absence of adjusted edges for square tabs and windows.

Indeed, even the lace menu has been restyled the rich looking, adjusted tabs repute with something that means to be much more practical.

Around there of the suite, there is almost no distinction to past renditions as far as the course of action and association of elements. On the off chance that you can move beyond the Metro restyle, Office 2013 is an exceptionally natural mammoth, a useful redesign of the past gathering of utilizations.

2.2 What Is Metro?

In the first place observed as the tile based UI and menu framework on Windows Telephone (discharged in 2010) the basic response to that portable framework's UI was sufficiently solid for Microsoft to move it out to different administrations.

Xbox 360 consoles were initially, trailed by the webmail framework Hotmail (restyled as Outlook.com) and after that came Windows 8. Office 2013 is quite recently the most recent in a long line of Microsoft items being restyled for finger centered collaboration between human and PC, made conceivable with touch screen gadgets.

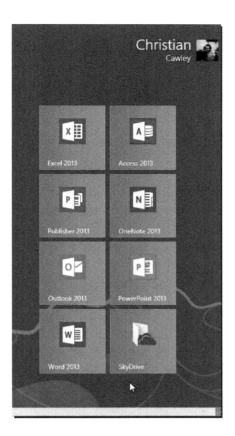

Obviously, not everybody possesses a touch screen gadget, so importantly the Metro UI (now renamed by Microsoft as "Current", notwithstanding the proceeded with utilization of the previous term by innovation columnists) can without much of a stretch be associated with by mouse and console.

Anyplace you see tiles, square lines and the WP Segos text style you can make sure that the Metro UI is being used somehow.

2.3 Practical Changes Since Office 2010

Microsoft Office 2013 isn't about the UI obviously it's about efficiency. Likewise with past discharges (that have additionally had UI amendments) Office 2013 components different useful changes, new elements expected to improve utilizing the product.

Different parts of the suite have had modifications and upgrades presented in Office 2013. Joint effort and comments, for example, is fundamentally modified especially in Word and PowerPoint. Somewhere else, the usage of Metro UI and the different tablet centered "touch modes" merit examining, if just for the fluctuated achievement they each accomplish.

Microsoft Get to be ostensibly the beneficiary of the most striking modifications, upgraded now for the making of program based applications that can be conveyed inside corporate systems running SharePoint or Office 365.

3. What You Need to Know about Word

Presumably the most imperative component of Microsoft Office for the lion's share of clients (and Microsoft!) is Word. The new form of the world's most loved word preparing device is pleasingly well known, in spite of the Metro trappings, and comes outfitted with some incredible new elements and amendments of more established components that additionally affirm its place in the hearts of organizations, schools and home clients all over the place.

Notwithstanding overhauled components and capacities, Word 2013 incorporates different new elements, for example, a read mode and the capacity to alter and audit PDFs.

3.1 Read Mode in Word 2013

Accessible by opening Perspective > Read Mode, this new element is intended to empower you to get a full site hit of the report that is unsullied by menus or other organizing devices. It may be thought to be especially suited to tablet gadgets; however in the event that your screen is equipped for showing a desktop turned vertically, you'll likewise observe some advantage.

Notwithstanding Read Mode, the full screen see has been safeguarded from the concealed menus (or its place on the Brisk Dispatch toolbar for some clients) and given another home in the upper right corner of the Word 2013 window. This is arguably not in the same class as the device in past forms, nonetheless, and renounces content just; catch free virtue for left and right sheets for any instruments that are dynamic.

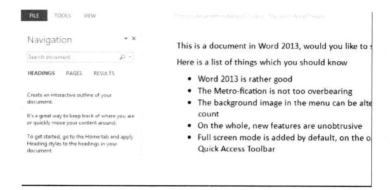

3.2 Finding New Layouts

A standout amongst the most imperative things that the in your face Microsoft Word client ought to comprehend is the creation and man agreement of formats. Word 2013 has another screen for making layouts, got to when you initially dispatch the application.

This "backstage" territory resembles an amalgamation of the Word 2010 Record menu and the new screen, displaying connections to late reports on the left and a determination of new formats on the privilege.

Here you'll locate a decent determination of as good as ever formats, covering everything from blog entries and much obliged offering solicitations to yearly reports and unrecorded music flyers. Actually these can all be altered as before to create work custom fitted to your own needs, and a pursuit apparatus at the highest point of the page gives access to formats on the web. Where appropriate, scan will show appropriate formats for different applications in the suite.

3.3 Propelled Archive Design

Support, spaces and content wrapping all keep on being available in Word 2013, however the path in which pictures or other inserted component can be put has been enhanced on account of the live format framework. This element enables you to left tap the picture before dragging it around the page, putting it precisely where you need.

Twitter v2 Explained

Content can be set to stream around, behind or in front as some time recently; however it is with the liquid situating of components that this feature truly emerges. Changes to wrapping can be made by the relevant fly up symbol that is shown (see picture).

While we're looking at implanting media, online pictures and recordings can at long last be installed into a Word archive in Office 2013, by means of the Embed tab.

3.4 Altering and looking into PDFs

While Microsoft spent so much time pushing its own record imaging framework, Adobe's PDF developed into the true standard. Thus, forms of Microsoft Office have been ease back to receive the document sort. Indeed, even Office 2007 was discharged

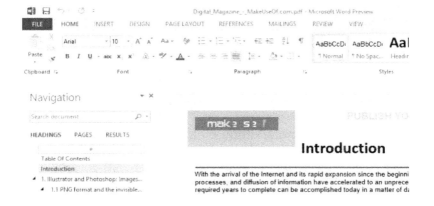

Introduction

With the arrival of the Internet and its rapid expansion since the beginni processes, and diffusion of information have accelerated to an unprece required years to complete can be accomplished today in a matter of da

Without the capacity to peruse and make PDFs until the arrival of Administration Pack 2.

Word 2013 expands on this by offering help for making and altering PDFs. Take note of those altering PDFs can be hit and miss the procedure requires that the current PDF archive is changed over into DOCX arrange, something that can bring about an off base design. Basic designs ought to change over without an excess of inconvenience, in any case.

Take note of that altering happens once the record is changed over to DOCX design, and all things considered you should choose the PDF document alternative in the Spare as discourse box to keep your progressions.

3.5 Upgrades to Coordinated effort

On the off chance that you consistently chip away at reports with others, at that point the enhancements to Microsoft Word's joint effort and audit instruments may demonstrate intriguing.

This amendment empowers significantly less demanding coordinated effort by including a rearranged increase view and support for cloud drives.

Both of these components empower a streamlined remarking framework, bringing about continuous input and talk inside the body of the report!

Dealing with remarks is so significantly less demanding. Let's assume you've been sent a record to survey; you can include a remark by highlighting the section and clicking Supplement > New Remark from the lace. Your musings can then be gone into the box with your name and picture showed, and consequent remarks will seem strung. Then tablet clients can make remarks utilizing a stylus, while the already moderate errand of remark evacuation in a completed draft is effectively done by scratching off every one thus.

3.6 Characterize and Get it

Likewise on the Survey tab you will locate another instrument to help with dialect and linguistic use. The Characterize capacity is propelled by choosing the word or entry and after that tapping the catch in the Sealing area of the lace menu or by squeezing CTRL+F7 and is utilized as a part of conjunction with worked in instruments or modules to increase additional comprehension of a word or reference.

On first utilization of this element, you might be incited to download a lexicon. Among those accessible is the Merriam Webster word reference.

4.   Does Excel Do Enough Already?

Did you realize that the reason for the main finish electronic spreadsheet programming (VisiCalc) was roused by a board based count? Or, on the other hand that Microsoft Office owes its reality to this application?

Microsoft Exceed expectations have made considerable progress since its underlying discharge on early Mac PCs as a contender to VisiCalc, however remains famously adaptable. It's being used differently as a period administration apparatus, database, measurable examination programming and a great deal more. Actually, it's amazing that Microsoft can keep on adding components to what is basically an including genius gram.

In any case, notwithstanding dangers from bad to the bone information investigation apparatuses, Microsoft makes enhancements to Exceed expectations that keep up the application's multi-reason flexibility. Exceed expectations 2013 incorporates a few redesigned capacities and elements.

4.1 Suggested Diagrams

Taking after the graph introduction changes of Exceed expectations 2007 and 2010, the new form gets rid of the emphasis on the outline wizard, rather offering the

Suggested Diagrams device. The route in which this works is entirely instinctive; a table with a basic design of two lines and four sections will bring about a recommendation of a straightforward outline, for example, a line bar.

In the interim a more muddled table will bring about the proposal of a more point by point outline, and the magnificence of this new suggestion framework is that you can pick an alternate diagram on the off chance that you don't care for the outcomes.

When entering a table, the Prescribed Outlines catch can be found on the Embed tab. Make sure to choose the table before tap the catch. In the event that your table elements a variety of information sorts, these can be covered up if essential using the Channel catch shown to one side of the outline in Graph Configuration see. This Graph Channels choice streamlines the way toward including and expelling information from a diagram with basic check boxes and furthermore empowers the exchanging of the outline plan in the vicinity of 2D and 3D.

You can likewise get some great responses from anybody seeing your graph by changing an incentive in your diagram's table the outline's adjustment to the new figures will be vivified, constantly extraordinary for the "goodness" consider.

(Take note of that online joint effort still isn't workable for Exceed expectations pay special mind to the paramount "Document is bolted" cautioning when you attempt to alter an officially open record.)

4.2 Speedy Examination

Presented in Exceed expectations 2007, contingent organizing empowers the client to apply arranging in view of the substance of the phone (a prime illustration may be shading the content red to speak to a misfortune).

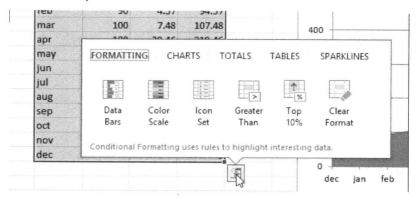

In Exceed expectations 2013, restrictive designing has been made simpler to apply, because of the Snappy Investigation symbol that shows up at the base right of a chose table or part of information. This empowers you to rapidly choose from a typical determination of contingent arranging, (for example, the case above). With this device you can likewise rapidly show aggregate figures, compute midpoints and include esteems your table.

4.3 Proposed PivotTables

Some time ago to be an ace of Exceed expectations you needed to comprehend PivotTables back to front. With Exceed expectations 2013 there is as yet a necessity to be acquainted with this element, yet another device, Recommended PivotTables, empowers easygoing clients to exploit the product's capacity to deal with interconnected information.

Like Recommended Diagrams, this component is anything but difficult to utilize. Once you've chosen your information, utilize the Embed tab to discover the Suggested PivotTables catch and watch the outcomes.

4.4 Power See for Power Clients

Inaccessible in the littler bundles is Power See, which comes as a feature of the Workplace Proficient In addition to adaptation of Exceed expectations. This instrument is Exceed expectations' key weapon in the fight against different business knowledge bundles, and can transform a tremendous table of numbers into striking, significant illustrations (for example, complex data with reference to areas maybe deals information can be shown by making utilization of Bing Maps).

The option of the Power Pivot includes transforms Exceed expectations into an application that can conceivably match fruitful business knowledge programming, for example, Business Objects.

5. PowerPoint 2013 A New Dimension

Consistently, in workplaces over the world, individuals are attempting to remain conscious in introductions.

This is infrequently the blame of the product, and quite often because of the bland substance and the capacity (or absence of!) of the speaker. Making introductions additionally convincing is a test that Microsoft sets itself with each new arrival of PowerPoint.

Throughout the years this has been endeavored with the expansion of implanted rich media and enhanced execution, and this time around Microsoft have conveyed upgrades to slide plan, new swipes and zooms and even another view.

5.1 Don't Alter With Fingers!

Something that you should remember with Office 2013 is that despite the fact that the new Metro style client between face is proposed for use by fingers, it isn't ideal for this utilization.

This is epitomized in PowerPoint 2013, where you ought to be extremely cautious about utilizing something besides the conventional mouse and console to make and alter new introductions. Components, for example, the window controls in the upper right, the zoom slider at the base and even the touch mode switch are cumbersome and hard to access with fingers.

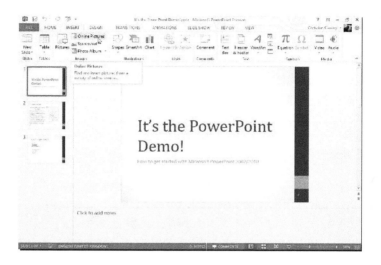

In the event that your tablet has a stylus, at that point utilize this; however surely don't depend on your fingers!

5.2 New Look Moderator See

On account of the Metro search for PowerPoint, Moderator See has a fresh out of the box new look. Gone for clients will's identity showing their introductions through a projector or huge display it offers an alternate view to the one being shown. The Moderator See empowers the client to prepare by showing notes about the slide and giving a see of the following, and offers different controls, including a pen device for attracting the gathering of people's thoughtfulness regarding a particular slide or detail.

Another Route network in Moderator See empowers you to effectively explore between slides, while Slide Zoom enables you to zoom into a slide either with the finger thumb "squeeze" signal or by tapping the mouse.

5.3 Swipes and Zooms in Introductions

Zooming and swiping is normal in PowerPoint 2013. For example, there is another exchange enclose that scopes from the right hand side of the screen, albeit inquisitively this isn't a plan component that is conveyed crosswise over Office 2013.

Despite the fact that the utilization of fingers for altering introductions is not exhorted (see above), review a PowerPoint introduction on a touch screen tablet conveys a radical new measurement to the completed item, empowering you to swipe left and ideal to explore through the introduction, squeeze or tap to zoom and general empowering you to concentrate on the introduction.

The potential outcomes of awing your group of onlookers by conveying a PowerPoint introduction through a handheld touch screen gadget are apparent!

5.4 Upgrades to Slide Outline

Despite the fact that there isn't anything extensively extraordinary in PowerPoint 2013, Microsoft has in any case acquainted a couple of helpful apparatuses with enhance the experience of making another introduction.

In case you're utilizing a cutting edge portable workstation or a tablet, the odds are that it is a widescreen gadget. New formats in 16:9 for tangle have been added to the application and to Office.com, and the assignment of adjusting slides has been streamlined as well. Subjects incorporated into PowerPoint 2013 accompanied a few variations, empowering you to change the shade of foundations, headings and different components. You can think about these adjustments as "sub subjects" and they add another measurement to making new introductions.

Somewhere else, Pictures, content boxes and different components can be effectively adjusted and masterminded on a slide by dragging them into place, and shading coordinating is made less demanding with the expansion of an eye dropper instrument.

You will have found in the segment about Microsoft Word 2013 that support for implanting on the web content has been included and the same is valid in PowerPoint 2013, with installing accessible on the Embed tab.

5.5 Joint effort Upgrades in PowerPoint 2013

Alongside the emphasis on the cloud (as clarified prior and in more detail in Section 8), PowerPoint 2013 brags an indistinguishable cooperation upgrades from Word.

Displayed in a fundamentally the same as way, the updated remarks are shown by a little discourse rise, with an arrangement for inline answers. In case you're utilizing PowerPoint 2013 in a corporate setting and have Lync introduced, the Nearness framework will fill you in regarding whether colleagues are accessible to visit. Not at all like Exceed expectations, has PowerPoint empowered numerous clients to take a shot at a similar introduction in the meantime with Sky Drive, a corporate system and PowerPoint Web Application as the source location.

The fantastic Present Online device has additionally experienced a modification; this makes it conceivable to webcast slideshows, and you can deal with these by means of the Moderator See.

6.   Microsoft Outlook - Redesigned

While its application in Windows Telephone and Windows 8 is shocking, Metro is a sensibly decent UI as a rule. Tragically for Standpoint 2013, the new look doesn't exactly work.

This is most obvious when seeing the messages list sheet, where refinement between the showed messages is not as much as clear.

Practically, in the interim, Viewpoint 2013 elements a couple of past due upgrades, for example, inline answers in messages and the greatly vaunted reconciliation with Microsoft's current securing, Skype. Shockingly, touch interface choices demonstrate troublesome with Viewpoint 2013 on a tablet/touch screen gadget, which is frustrating given how effortlessly a similar group of elements are gotten to on a Windows Telephone.

While the symbols in the lower left corner have been supplanted with Metro sequel catches for Mail, Date book, Individuals and Errands, whatever remains of the interface is restricted to the topic picked when you at first setup Office 2013.

6.1 Inline Answers in Your Inbox

Customarily, in Viewpoint, answers must be composed in another window, actuated when the Answer catch was clicked. With Viewpoint 2013 this has been updated (finally!) to empower messages to be answered to inside the Perusing Sheet.

This spares some time, as do the greater part of upgrades in the email see. Many individuals select to erase messages once read, and this has been made substantially less complex in Viewpoint 2013 with the arrangement of a relevant Erase catch that shows up when the mouse is drifting over a message.

Modifications to the new mail warnings (in Windows 8, this is coordinated with the working framework's own notice framework) result in less data, and no choice to erase messages.

6.2 Timetable Changes

The helpful logbook review shown in the Viewpoint 2010 inbox see stays in Standpoint 2013, while the Schedule name now shows imminent arrangements when the mouse is drifted over it.

In general, in any case, little has changed in the date-book itself, which takes a large portion of its refresh lines from Viewpoint. Come. Subsequently, climate symbols show up along a strip underneath the lace menu while the present time of day is indicated by a shaded strip over the Day by day and Week after week sees.

6.3 Individuals Are Contacts

Another Windows 8 impact is the renaming of the Viewpoint contacts rundown to Individuals. In Viewpoint

Christian-Mark Cawley

CONTACT   NOTES   WHAT'S NEW

Calendar
Schedule a meeting

Profile
Outlook (Contacts)

Send Email
atomickarma@cmcawley.co.uk

Send Email
christian@cmcawley.co.uk

2013 it copies the working framework application, bringing together contacts from LinkedIn, Face book and Windows Live, and empowers the extra unification of copies into a solitary card.

Moreover, top picks from your Kin rundown can be added to the to do bar on the right hand of the Standpoint window (alongside the schedule review) which is valuable for checking their status or whereabouts.

6.4 Don't Touch It!

Like PowerPoint, Standpoint 2013 components a supposed touch mode, yet this is baffling. In any case, the little drop down menu used to begin touch mode requires the utilization of a mouse to get to it!

When actuated, Standpoint's touch mode is minimal more than a streamlined rendition of the principle application, with the expansion of a white fringe around different components and some alternate way catches at the edge of the screen.

With everything taken into account, as touch accommodating applications go, Standpoint 2013 isn't close by anyone's standards. Different touch signals for example, Date book view's squeeze to zoom, which switches between day, week and month function admirably, however Standpoint's usefulness is left needing in touch mode.

In the event that utilizing Office 2013 on a Windows 8 tablet you may be in an ideal situation depending on the local Mail, Date book and Individuals applications…

7.   The Secret Weapon: OneNote

Seemingly the most underrated application in the Microsoft Office suite, OneNote 2013 components some helpful upgrade ments including an option adaptation for tablets.

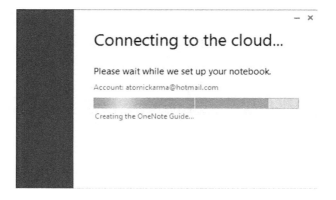

In case you're not utilizing OneNote as of now you should think of it as. Microsoft has discharged renditions of this cloud adjusted note taking application for all mainstream portable stages, and its adaptability is with the end goal that on the off chance that you haven't attempted it as of now you'll probe capably continue backpedaling to it once you do!

7.1 Making Noticed the OneNote Way

Initially presented in Office 2003, OneNote has advanced deliberately throughout the years, achieving its present condition of Sky Drive dependent synchronizing scratch pad that can be gotten to from Windows Telephones (and other cell phones).

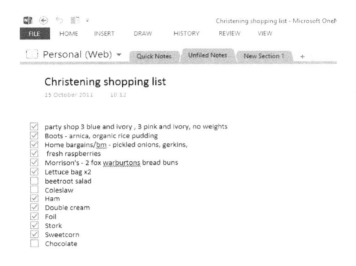

In OneNote 2013 there has been a slight redesign of key devices however little to demonstrate a discount reexamine of the application.

Making notes is simple on account of the vast note pad segment of the screen, while route through note pads can be performed by means of another dropdown menu that shows up by means of a bolt underneath the scratch pad title.

7.2 Inserting Spreadsheets

Likely the most prominent expansion to OneNote accompanies the enhanced spreadsheet device, which empowers you to make Exceed expectations tables inside journal pages. This is hotly anticipated change on the past tablet instrument, and existing Exceed expectations records can be inserted and altered, another late change.

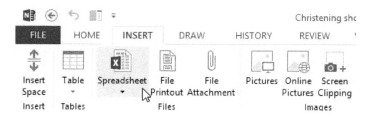

It's not simply Exceed expectations that can be discovered inserted in OneNote Visio graphs can likewise show up in your notes, with ongoing, moment alters accessible, just by double tapping the implanted chart, propelling the primary application and sparing.

7.3 OneNote MX

Touch in OneNote 2013 comes in two flavors. For standard utilize, the modest Fast Get to Toolbar again gives access to the Touch Mode catch, and as with Viewpoint 2013 the implantation is of the slapdash, amplification and dispersing out assortment.

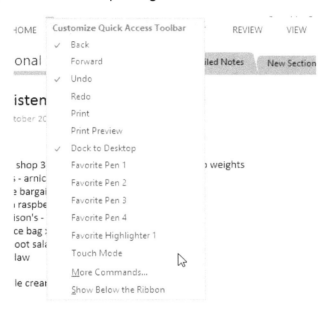

Be that as it may, OneNote 2013 games somewhat of astonishment in the state of a different application called OneNote MX. This is particularly a touch based application, including a round menu framework that uses arranging controls. A solitary tap of the word or expression that requires altering shows an on screen catch those outcomes in the menu, which astutely offers air conditioning cuss to a wide choice of controls in a constrained space.

OneNote MX additionally highlights a valuable strategy for exploring through note pads, areas and pages by dragging them out in boards from the left half of the screen.

In the same class as this appears to be, OneNote MX isn't great. Of course, it's a stage in the correct bearing, and you'll be unable to utilize your fingers to configuration message in the standard OneNote with such proficiency, yet tragically there are a couple key angles missing from this form, for example, the capacity to record sound notes and the valuable content in-photographs acknowledgment apparatus.

8. Office 2013 and SkyDrive

Another key part of Office 2013 that is impressively unique in relation to past adaptations of the profitability suite is the incorporation with Sky Drive, Microsoft's distributed storage framework.

Office

Meet SkyDrive.

Signing in to Office means you can save documents to the cloud with Microsoft SkyDrive.

SkyDrive gives you anywhere access to your files and makes it easy to share them with family and friends.

Your files are saved online at SkyDrive.com and also to the SkyDrive folder on your PC, so you can work offline and your changes will sync when you reconnect.

Next

An ever increasing number of administrations have been joined into Sky Drive in the course of recent months, from Windows 8 profiles to reports made in Microsoft Office Web Applications, so it ought to shock no one to discover that Sky Drive is a capacity choice when you make and spare documents.

Truth be told, Sky Drive is the default stockpiling decision, regardless of whether you have an online Windows account or not.

8.1 Joining with SkyDrive

Office 2013, similar to the new Windows, includes close combination with Microsoft's free distributed storage benefit Sky Drive. It's that close that you generally know when you're marked in, and in spite of the fact that leeway for some, you may favor not to have your reports consequently spared to the cloud.

There are two approaches to sign into Office 2013, by means of a Microsoft record, (for example, Hotmail, Windows Live or even Xbox Live) or utilizing a system represent a school or business. Just the previous will give access to Sky Drive, be that as it may (the last giving access to nearby distributed storage, maybe through SharePoint).

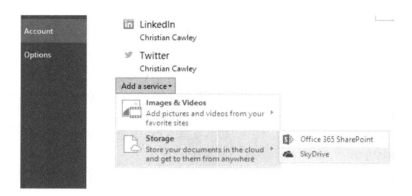

In any of the Workplace applications, changing to the Document tab and opening Records shows the different administrations and records related with your profile. In case you're utilizing Windows 8 these may be abundant. You may see an Expel alternative take note of this must be utilized if there is another client account setup on the PC being referred to.

Notwithstanding, you can keep Sky Drive from being the default spare area. This is effectively arranged by means of Record > Choices > Spare, where the check against dependably indicate "Sign into Sky Drive area" amid Spare ought to be cleared.

9. The Rest of Microsoft Office

Contingent upon which adaptation of Microsoft Office you buy, you'll additionally have the capacity to access the more propelled instruments, for example, Get to, InfoPath, Lync, Venture and Visio.

These devices are incorporated into the more costly accumulations, and are gone for little and medium estimated organizations that require databases, texting, extend administration, outlining and electronic shape plan.

They're not gone for understudies (in spite of the fact that Microsoft Get to might demonstrate helpful to numerous) and accordingly we're just going to cover the key updates acquainted with each bundle in Microsoft Office 2013.

9.1 Get to

Microsoft's famous desktop database administration application Get to is utilized for errands as assorted as finance to running sites. This new form includes some intriguing new components alongside the new look Metro interface.

Program based database applications can be manufactured and sent through Office 365 or a corporate SharePoint server, with the choice to include predesigned table formats. Information can be foreign made from different hotspots for these applications, which can be effortlessly propelled/sent from the Record menu.

9.2 Distributer

On the off chance that the components of Microsoft Word aren't sufficient to empower you to deliver the kind of archives that you need, Small scale delicate Distributer 2013 might have the capacity to offer assistance.

As a desktop distributing application, Distributer is gone for private companies without the assets for an outline pro or a duplicate of QuarkXPress. The absence of similarity with this and Adobe InDesign keep on making Distributer one of Microsoft's few specialty items; the Bar arrange can't be opened in other Microsoft applications or other office suites, for example.

Constraints aside, Distributer has been broadly utilized as a part of independent company workplaces and the most recent form includes some new features and another look. Alongside the normal Metro fiction of the UI, extra impacts, for example, shadows, shines, and reflections can be added to content, pictures and shapes, with new preset styles that can be set with a solitary snap. Once more, pictures from the web can be included, and pictures can be set as page foundations.

There's an inclination with Distributer that you may have the capacity to accomplish far beyond with prior variants obviously, this will rely on upon your creative energy...

9.3 Office 2013 Applications for Corporate Clients

Notwithstanding the standard applications that ship with the fundamental forms of Microsoft Office 2013, there are extra parts, for example, InfoPath, Lync, Venture and Visio.

Rules and restrictive organizing are among the new elements in InfoPath 2013, alongside support for a wide assortment of database configurations.

The most recent rendition of the corporate online delivery person Microsoft Lync highlights a choice of changes to its collaboration devices, utilizing whiteboard archives and PowerPoint introductions. Desktop and application sharing is additionally conceivable through Lync.

Microsoft has dodged any significant updates to Venture 2013 other than the Metro UI and the expansion of Venture Portfolio Administration, an adaptable, online instrument that can be utilized to oversee ventures "live" from various gadgets as opposed to depending on the more static, custom interface.

At long last we have Microsoft Visio 2013. With less demanding making of charts, enhanced synchronous joint effort and touch bolster, Visio 2013 empowers the connecting of graph shapes to ongoing information, unleashing the energy of the application as another measurable device. Outlines can be shared through the program with Office 365 and SharePoint, and the device underpins the most recent charting principles.

10. Office 2013 Should You Upgrade?

At this point you ought to have a thought of how to get to the most imperative new capacities added to the Microsoft Office suite, have dealt with the Metro UI and increased some comprehension of the utilization of SkyDrive as a distributed storage framework in Office 2013.

The unavoidable issue, obviously, is whether you ought to be set up to part with your well deserved money for the suite (or even individual segments).

Wrapping things up.

You can use Office now — but please stay online as we make some finishing touches.

All things considered, how about we consider the realities. As a matter of first importance, this is the primary form of Microsoft Office to offer a cloud based membership adaptation to standard clients in the state of Office 365. Tragically, it is additionally inconsistent with Windows XP and Windows Vista. This implies just clients running Windows 7 and Windows 8 PCs will have the capacity to take advantage of the new elements.

In the interim, in case you're not a devotee of the Metro UI then you're presumably going to be disappointed by Office 2013.

With everything taken into account, this is a decent move up to Microsoft Office that ticks the greater part of the privilege boxes yet doesn't generally offer much in the method for new "executioner" includes that may force you to redesign.

Similarly as with any product buy, a ultimate conclusion is dependent upon you. On the off chance that you feel that there are sufficient new components to legitimize a redesign and you're running Windows 7 or Windows 8 then Office 2013 ought to suit you. Be that as it may, in case you're more joyful with Windows XP and needn't bother with SkyDrive mix then past forms of Microsoft Office or a totally vary end suite may be your inclination.

11. Appendix

1. System Requirements

Every rendition of Microsoft Office requires a framework with a higher least framework determination, and Office 2013 is the same. Framework necessities for Microsoft Office 2013 are as per the following.

Processor	1GHz or greater x86/x64 Processor with SSE2 instruction set
Memory	1GB RAM (32 Bit), 2GB RAM (64 Bit)
Hard Disk Space	3.0 GB free disk space
Display	1024 x 576 resolution or higher

Then, designs equipment speeding up requires a DirectX10 good illustrations card, and Microsoft Office 2013 will keep running on Windows 7, Windows 8 , Windows Server 2008 R2 and Windows Server 2012.

Processor aside, the arrival of Microsoft Office for Windows RT gadgets, (for example, the Surface RT) has the same sys-tem specs.

2. Introducing Office 2013

On the off chance that you've bought a standard plate duplicate of Microsoft Office 2013, establishment will be clear, specifically from the optical media.

Then again, on the off chance that you've joined to Office 365, establishment will be by means of a download from the web. One preferred standpoint of this is you will have the capacity to begin utilizing a portion of the applications before establishment has finished helpful in case you're in a surge! Full subtle elements and a free trial can be found Microsoft website, where you will likewise discover data about the membership alternatives for Office 365, which begin at $6 a month.

3. Office Web Applications

Like the desktop variant of Microsoft Office 2013, the Workplace Web Applications have been restyled with the Metro UI.

Microsoft Office Web Applications can be gotten to through most programs; essentially sign into a Windows Live/Hotmail account at SkyDrive as to begin utilizing the online forms of Word, Exceed expectations, OneNote or PowerPoint.

While the components on offer aren't as far reaching as those in the desktop applications, these web apparatuses by and by offer an impressive preferred standpoint to anybody wanting to run a home or little office on a tight spending plan they're completely allowed to utilize! Records made and altered with Office Web Applications are naturally put away to SkyDrive.